ANIMALS
ANIMALS

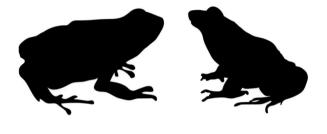

FROGS

BY MARTIN SCHWABACHER

BENCHMARK BOOKS

MARSHALL CAVENDISH
NEW YORK

Series Consultant
James Doherty
General Curator, Bronx Zoo, New York

Thanks to Deborah Behler, Wildlife Conservation Society, Bronx, New York, for her expert reading of this manuscript.

Benchmark Books
Marshall Cavendish
99 White Plains Road
Tarrytown, NY 10591–9001
www.marshallcavendish.com

Maps by Ian Warpole

Library of Congress Cataloging-in-Publication Data

Schwabacher, Martin.
Frogs / by Martin Schwabacher.
p. cm. – (Animals animals)
Summary: Describes the physical characteristics, behavior, habitat, and
endangered status of the frog.
Includes bibliographical references and index.
ISBN 0-7614-1619-6
1. Frogs–Juvenile literature. [1. Frogs. 2. Endangered species.]
I.Title. II. Series.

QL668.E2S39 2004
597.8'9–dc22
2003013124

Photo Research by Anne Burns Images

Cover Photo by Animals Animals/Henry Ausloos

The photographs in this book are used with permission and through the courtesy of:
Animals Animals: Robert Lubeck, 4; Patti Murray, 6–7; Leach OSF, 8; Zig Leszczynski, 10, 15, 22; Stephen Dalton, 16 (right); Michael Fogden, 17 (left), 38; OSF 17 (top right); Dani/Jeske 17 (bottom); S. Dalton, OSF, 20; Breck P.Kent, 30, 31, 32; Ingrid Van Den Berg, 36; Barbara Reed, 40–41; Michael Thompson, 42. *Corbis*: George D.Lepp, 13 (top); Joe McDonald, 13 (bottom); Jim Zuckerman, 16 (top); Nigel J.Dennis, 16 (bottom); Rod Patterson/Gallo Images, 18; Michael & Patricia Fogden, 24–25, 28; Maryann McDonald, 33; David Aubrey, 35.

Printed in China

1 3 5 6 4 2

CONTENTS

1

INTRODUCING FROGS

Imagine if a fish could grow legs and climb out of the water–and then start breathing air. This may be impossible for fish, but it is exactly what most frogs do as a normal part of growing up.

Frogs are *amphibians*–animals that spend the first part of their life underwater, and then switch to breathing air. When young frogs first come out of their eggs, they look like tiny fish. They have *gills* that let them breathe under-water, as fish do. They have no legs, and they swim by wiggling their tails back and forth. At this age they are known as *tadpoles* or *polliwogs*. But then their bodies begin to change. The tadpoles' gills and tail slowly disappear, and they grow four legs.

A frog's front legs are very short and skinny, but the back legs are big and strong. An adult frog's back legs are as long as its whole body.

BULLFROGS SUN THEMSELVES ON A MOSSY ROCK. NORTH AMERICA'S LARGEST NATIVE FROG, THE BULLFROG CAN MEASURE UP TO 6 INCHES (15 CM) IN LENGTH.

MANY FROGS, LIKE THESE YOUNG
GREEN FROGS, ALWAYS STAY
CLOSE TO WATER.

IN GENERAL, THE LONGER A FROG'S HIND LEGS ARE, THE BETTER A LEAPER IT IS.

This is why frogs are such great jumpers. They fold up their powerful hind legs underneath them in thirds, like a Z. To jump, they suddenly unfold their legs. As their legs straighten, the frog is launched into the air.

Sometimes instead of jumping, a frog will run or skitter on four legs. Some frogs can skitter along the surface of water.

Most frogs are also good swimmers. Their back feet have webs between the toes, like ducks' feet. When swimming, frogs fold and then straighten their legs to push off against

8

the water. This style of swimming is known as the frog kick when people do it.

While frogs spend some time swimming, most of their day is spent out of the water, hunting and keeping warm. Frogs are cold–blooded, meaning their bodies alone cannot keep them warm. To keep warm, frogs have to absorb the warmth of their surroundings. Many frogs do this by climbing up on rocks to sunbathe, keeping close to a water source. If a frog dries out, it can quickly lose half its weight and die. Most frogs either stay near water or keep moist with rain or dew, or by burrowing in damp soil. When they are not near water, a slimy coating keeps their skin damp.

All frogs have many things in common, but what makes them truly fascinating are their differences. A great variety of frogs can be found all over the world.

2
A WORLD OF FROGS

Frogs come in many different shapes, sizes, and colors. In all, there are more than 4,800 *species*, or kinds, of frogs and toads. In general, frogs are smooth and moist with long hind legs. While both frogs and toads are amphibians, they are different in a number of ways. The easiest way to tell them apart is by looking at their skin. Toads have dry skin that is often covered with bumpy warts. Toads also walk or hop rather than jump, and live farther from water than do most frogs.

The most common frog in North America is the leopard frog, which is green, brown, or gray, with black spots. The largest North American frog is the bullfrog. Bullfrogs can grow up to 8 inches (20 cm) long–18 inches (46 cm) with their legs stretched out–and weigh well over a pound (0.5 kg). The largest frog in the world, the African giant frog, grows to nearly a foot long (30 cm). It can stretch to 26 inches (66 cm) and can weigh up to 10 pounds (4.5 kg).

ORNATE HORNED FROGS OF SOUTH AMERICA HAVE MOUTHS AS WIDE AS THEIR HEADS. IT IS SAID THAT THESE LARGE FROGS WILL EAT ANYTHING THAT MOVES. IN FACT, THEY DO HAVE HEARTY APPETITES AND EAT SNAKES, LIZARDS, AND MICE, AMONG OTHER THINGS.

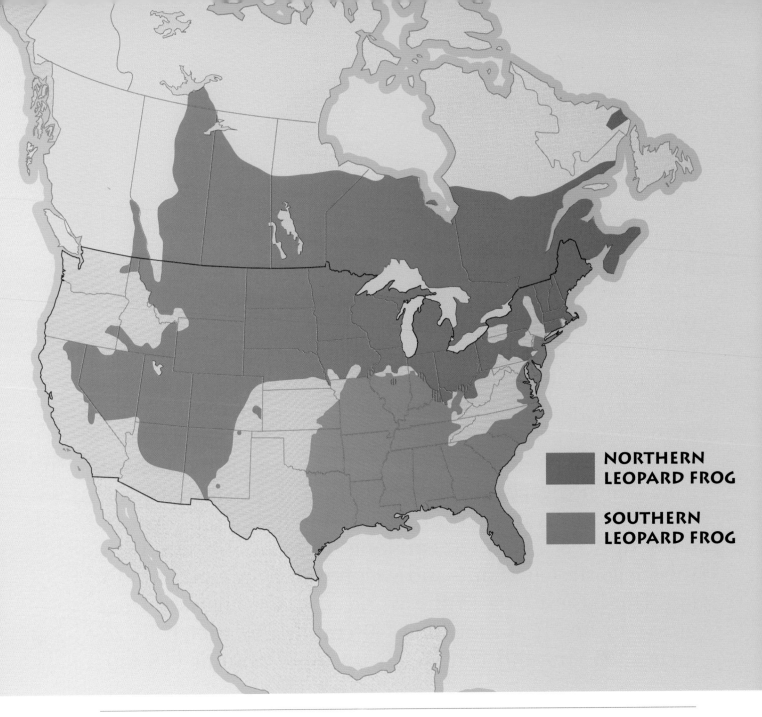

NORTHERN
LEOPARD FROG

SOUTHERN
LEOPARD FROG

LEOPARD FROGS ARE THE MOST COMMON NORTH AMERICAN SPECIES. THIS MAP SHOWS WHERE NORTHERN AND SOUTHERN LEOPARD FROGS LIVE.

NORTHERN (ABOVE) AND SOUTHERN (BELOW) LEOPARD FROGS ARE ALMOST IDENTICAL. TO TELL THEM APART, LOOK FOR A LIGHT SPOT AT THE CENTER OF THE FROG'S EARDRUM, WHICH IS LOCATED RIGHT BEHIND THE EYE. SOUTHERN LEOPARD FROGS HAVE THIS SPOT. NORTHERN LEOPARD FROGS DO NOT.

The smallest frogs, such as the Brazilian gold frog, measure just 3/8 inch (1 cm).

Frogs live in warm, moist habitats all over the world. They can be found in most freshwater ponds, lakes, rivers, marshes, and streams. But some frogs manage to survive in drier places, such as forests, grasslands, mountains, and even the dry deserts of Africa. In places with hot, dry summers, some frogs bury themselves in the sand to wait out the heat.

Some frogs live mostly in water, while others hop through the grass or dig burrows in the dirt. But many frogs live in trees. Tree frogs are usually small, slim, and brightly colored. On their feet, they have sticky pads that help them to climb.

Between their legs, some tree frogs have flaps of skin that they spread out like wings. Though they are called flying frogs, they cannot actually fly, but they can glide as far as 50 feet (15 meters). Other tree frogs float softly to the ground, using their webbed, fanlike feet as a parachute.

Frogs come in just about every color. Many are hard to see because they are the same color as the plants next to them, or *camouflaged*. Frogs that live among leaves and grass are often green. Frogs that spend a lot of time on brown rocks may be brown.

AN AMAZON HORNED FROG HIDES AMONG LEAVES.

FROG SPECIES
HERE ARE A FEW TYPES OF FROGS FOUND AROUND THE WORLD.

AFRICAN BULLFROG
These frogs can measure up to 9 inches (23 cm) and weigh as much as 2 pounds (0.9 kg).

WALLACE'S FLYING FROG
MALAYSIA AND BORNEO
These frogs do not actually fly, but their webbed feet help them to glide.

TOMATO FROG
MADAGASCAR
These brightly colored frogs are not poisonous. They burrow into the ground and eat whatever insects happen to pass by.

YELLOW COMMON FROG
GREAT BRITAIN, EUROPE AND NORTHWESTERN ASIA
These frogs live as far north as the Arctic circle in Scandinavia.

LEAF FROG
SOUTHEAST ASIA
Its leaflike appearance makes this frog impossible to see on the forest floor unless it moves.

BLUE-JEANS POISON DART FROG
CENTRAL AMERICA
These tiny frogs measure only 1 to 2 inches (2.5–5 cm) when fully grown.

AN AFRICAN BULLFROG BURIES ITSELF IN THE SAND OF THE KALAHARI DESERT.

Some frogs can change color to match their surroundings. Their skin may be green when they hide in the grass, and then change to brown when they sit on a rock. This keeps them safe because they do not stand out against either background.

Other kinds of frogs do not blend in with their background at all. They have shockingly bright colors, often in eye-catching patterns. Instead of being hard to see, they have a different defense: they are poisonous. Their bright colors are a warning to other animals to stay away.

Poison dart frogs, for instance, have patterns of black with red, yellow, orange, pink, green, or blue. These frogs release poison through their skin. Any animal that eats one will get sick. In South America traditional hunters catch these frogs to make poison darts. To collect the poison, they rub the tip of the dart on the frog's back. Then they hunt by shooting the darts through blowguns. A blowgun is a long tube, like a straw used for shooting spitballs, only bigger.

Most frogs cannot fly, change color, or release poison. But all frogs have unusual features that are very different from those of other animals.

3
FROG BODIES

A frog sits quietly, waiting for an unsuspecting insect to fly by. Then suddenly the frog's tongue flicks out, catching a mosquito in midair. This flick of the tongue can happen too quickly for the human eye to follow.

Frogs have sticky tongues that are as long as their body. The tongues of many frogs are attached to the front of their mouth, not the back, which allows the tongue to stick out farther. The tip of their tongue is so sticky that if it touches a small animal, the animal gets stuck and cannot escape.

Frogs do not use their teeth to chew their food and only bite other animals when frightened. Instead, they use their teeth to keep animals in their mouth after they have caught them with their tongue.

A frog's eyes bulge out of its head. They stick out so far that a frog can swim underwater with only its eyes above

A FROG DIVES HEADFIRST INTO THE WATER.

the surface. This lets the frog look around while the rest of its body is hidden. One eye faces to the left and the other to the right, so that it can see all the way around its body.

Frogs have two sets of eyelids. The lower eyelid is clear, like swimming goggles, and covers the frog's eyes when it is underwater. Above the water, the frog keeps its eyes

THIS CLOSE-UP OF A BULLFROG'S EYE SHOWS THE CLEAR LOWER EYELID.

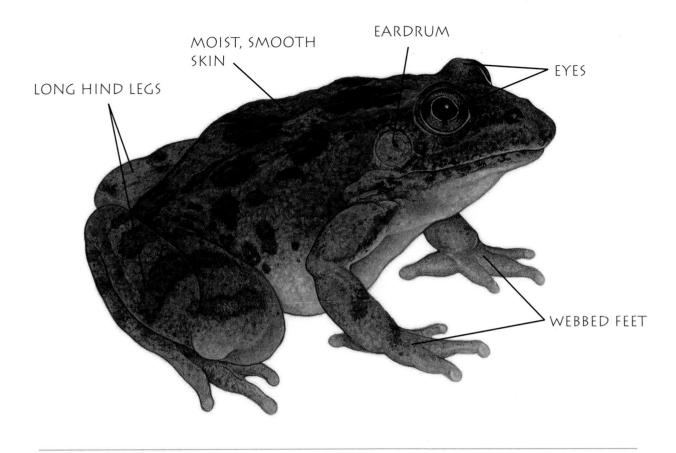

LONG HIND LEGS

MOIST, SMOOTH SKIN

EARDRUM

EYES

WEBBED FEET

LEOPARD FROG BODY

moist by blinking its clear eyelids. Frogs also blink to swallow food. Blinking pushes the eyes down into its head, which pushes down on the food in its mouth and helps it to swallow.

If you ever pick up a frog, you will notice that it feels soft and squishy, like a water balloon. This is because frogs have no ribs. Most *vertebrates*, or animals with back-bones, have bony ribs that make a hard case around their chest, but frogs do not.

MOST TREE FROGS HAVE
STICKY PADS ON THEIR TOES
TO HELP THEM CLING TO
BRANCHES AND LEAVES.

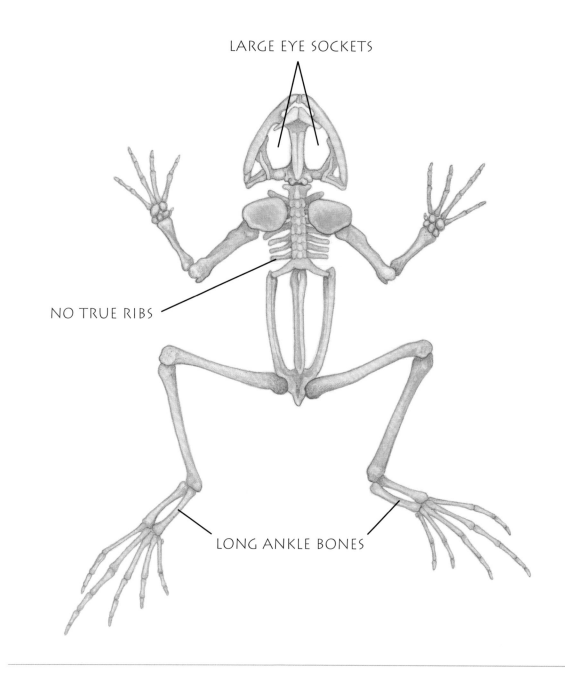

LARGE EYE SOCKETS

NO TRUE RIBS

LONG ANKLE BONES

FROG SKELETON

26

Frogs have many different ways of breathing. One method is to close their mouth and push air into their lungs. If you watch a frog closely, you may see this. But it happens very fast, like a quick gulp, and they do it only once or twice a minute. But frogs can breathe without taking any air into their lungs. Some breathe through the roof of their mouth, and most can obtain oxygen through their skin—even underwater.

More amazing than any single part of a frog's body, however, are the remarkable changes that take place as a frog grows from egg to adult.

4

A FROG'S LIFE

A frog's life starts when a female frog lays an egg. Some frogs lay a few dozen eggs, but others lay 10,000 eggs at a time. Frog eggs are round, and most are partly clear. Most frogs lay a whole mass of eggs that stick together in a large cluster, often at the bottom of a pond. Most frog eggs are very small–between 1/64– and 1/4-inch (1– and 5–mm) in diameter. Sometimes the eggs are tied by stringy fibers to grass or twigs. In some cases, they are stuck to a leaf above the water. When the eggs hatch, the young tadpoles drop into the water below.

Most frog eggs hatch in less than two weeks. When the tiny tadpoles first come out of their eggs, some glue themselves to the egg mass for a while so they are not washed away. As the tadpoles grow, they tend to swim in a group. They are safer in a group, and they can stir up

FROG EGGS CAN TAKE ANYWHERE FROM TWO DAYS TO SIX WEEKS TO HATCH.

MOST FROGS LAY LARGE GROUPS OF EGGS IN STANDING WATER.

more food by swimming together. The main food of tad-poles is algae–tiny plants that grow in water. Some algae float on the surface and some grow on rocks, where tad-poles scrape them off with their mouths.

Tadpoles eat a lot. To become an adult frog they must grow fifty times bigger and heavier. The whole process

TADPOLES LOOK MORE LIKE FISH THAN LIKE FROGS.

can take up to two years. In addition to growing legs, tadpoles need to grow many new organs, such as a stomach and lungs, and a whole new skeleton.

The first new limbs to appear on a tadpole are the back legs. Then front legs poke out of the skin near the head and the tail shrinks. By the time the frog can breathe air and climb out of the water, all four legs are fully grown,

31

but it has not yet lost all of its tail.

As the frog grows, its outer skin stretches and peels off. A new layer of skin underneath replaces the old skin. This is called *molting*. Frogs molt many times during the year. They pull their old skin over their head with their

32

ONCE IT IS ABLE TO BREATHE AIR THE YOUNG FROG CLIMBS OUT OF THE WATER. ITS TAIL IS STILL VISIBLE BUT WILL EVENTUALLY DISAPPEAR.

front legs. Most frogs eat the old skin after they shed it.

Adult frogs are carnivores, which means that they eat live *prey*. Their most common victims are flies, mosquitoes, and dragonflies, but they also eat caterpillars, slugs, spiders, and earthworms. Some frogs also catch small fish,

33

small frogs and tadpoles, or even birds. The American pickerel frog eats snails and crayfish, and the Brazilian horned frog will even eat mice and rats. But the main food of most frogs is insects, which make up about 80 percent of a frog's diet.

Tree frogs have been know to leap 10 feet (3 meters)–forty times their body length–to catch an insect. But most larger frogs hunt by sitting still and ambushing insects that pass by. Many frogs hardly move around at all and spend most of their lives in one small area. Each frog may have its own little part of the pond where it always sits. Some frogs get into wrestling matches to defend their private hunting spots.

As the seasons change, frogs must adapt to the changing weather. In places with hot, dry summers, some frogs bury themselves in the sand to wait out the heat. In places with very cold winters, frogs bury themselves in the mud at the bottom of ponds to *hibernate*–a form of rest deeper than sleep. Their heart rate slows down to less than one beat per minute. Their breathing nearly stops, too. Hibernating frogs use so little energy that they can go without a breath of air all winter. They absorb all the oxygen they need through their skin.

Spring or early summer is mating season for frogs.

A FROG MOVES IN ON ITS LUNCH.

ONLY MALE FROGS HAVE VOCAL SACS.

During mating season male frogs gather in large groups, or choruses, and sing loudly together. Each species of frog has a different song. The females find males of their own species by listening for the right song.

Frog songs are surprisingly loud. They range from the deep, low sounds of a bullfrog to the high, shrill calls of a spring peeper. Frogs do not need to open their mouths to sing. Instead, they pass air back and forth between their lungs and mouth. They can even sing underwater this way.

To make their calls louder, frogs blow up a large bubble of skin in their throat. Some species have one on each side of their throat. These large sacs of air make the frog songs louder, in the same way that a large drum makes a louder sound than a small drum.

Sometimes frogs will take turns and fit their calls into a pattern. By singing together, choruses of male frogs attract more females. Frogs also produce sounds to warn each other of danger. In many ways the songs of frogs are as beautiful and complex as are those of birds.

5
FROGS AND PEOPLE

Millions of frogs are used each year by people for food and medical research. But this is not the greatest danger people pose to frogs. A bigger problem is the loss of wild places where frogs can live. More than half of all *wetlands* in America have already been destroyed because people drained them to build houses, buildings, and farms.

But even where wild wetlands remain, frogs are still disappearing. Frogs are very sensitive to pollution, partly because they soak up water through their skin. Adding acid to the water where frogs live can kill them. Coal–burning power plants and other smoky factories create *acid rain*, harming many frogs.

Frogs are also threatened by other dangerous pollu–tion, including chemicals used for farming. Farmers use chemicals to kill weeds and harmful insects and to help plants grow. Rain washes these chemicals into rivers and ponds, poisoning frogs.

HABITAT DESTRUCTION MEANS TROUBLE FOR MANY ANIMALS OF THE RAIN FOREST, INCLUDING THE POISON DART FROG.

WHITE'S TREE FROGS ARE OFTEN KEPT AS PETS. THEY ARE ALSO KNOWN AS DUMPY TREE FROGS OR SMILING FROGS.

BECAUSE BULLFROGS CAN BE HELPFUL BY EATING HARMFUL INSECTS, PEOPLE
INTRODUCE THEM TO NEW AREAS. BUT SINCE BULLFROGS EAT NEARLY ANY-
THING THEY CAN SWALLOW, THEY CAN BE A THREAT TO THE ANIMALS
ALREADY LIVING THERE

All over North America, the number of frogs has dropped sharply since the 1980s. More and more frogs are also showing up with strange deformities, such as missing eyes or three legs. No one knows all of the reasons for this, but pollution is one cause. Stronger regulations against pollution are needed to protect wild places and help frogs and other animals survive.

acid rain: Rain that contains acid from air pollution.

amphibians: Animals that are born in the water and live on land when fully grown.

camouflaged: Hidden by matching the color of the surroundings.

gills: Parts of an animal's body that are used for breathing underwater.

hibernate: To spend the winter in a form of rest deeper than sleep.

molting: The shedding of an animal's outer layer of skin.

polliwogs: Another name for tadpoles.

prey: Animal that is hunted and eaten by other animals.

species: A certain kind of animal or plant.

tadpoles: Young frogs or toads that have not yet changed into their adult form and that look like small fish.

vertebrates: Animals having a backbone and a bony skeleton.

wetlands: Areas of land that are partly underwater, such as swamps or marshes.

BOOKS

Cassie, Brian. *National Audubon Society First Field Guide: Amphibians.* New York: Scholastic, 1999.

Coborn, John. *Frogs and Toads as a New Pet.* Neptune City, NJ: T.F.H. Publications, 1992.

Gibbons, Gail. *Frogs.* New York: Holiday House, 1993.

Greenberg, Daniel A. *Frogs.* Tarrytown, NY: Benchmark Books, 2001.

Grossman, Patricia. *Very First Things to Know About Frogs.* New York: Workman Publishing, 1999.

Hawes, Judy. *Why Frogs are Wet* New York: HarperCollins, 2000.

Long, Kim. Frogs: *A Wildlife Handbook.* Boulder, CO: Johnson Books, 1999.

Parsons, Harry. *The Nature of Frogs.* Vancouver: New York: Greystone, 2000.

Patent, Dorothy Hinshaw. *Flashy, Fantastic Rain Forest Frogs.* New York: Walker and Company, 1997.

White, William, Jr. *All About the Frog.* New York: Sterling, 1992.

Zoehfeld, Kathleen Weidner. *From Tadpole to Frog.* New York: Scholastic, 2002.

FIND OUT MORE

CDs

Elliott, Lang. *The Calls of Frogs and Toads.* Ithaca: NatureSound Studio, 1998.

WEB SITES

About amphibians

www.yahooligans.com/content/animals/amphibians/

All About Frogs: facts, jokes, and games

www.allaboutfrogs.org/froglnd.shtml

Exploratorium science museum for children

www.exploratorium.edu/frogs/

Frog calls

www.naturesound.com/frogs/frogs.html

Frogs!

www.pca.state.mn.us/kids/frogsforkids.html

ABOUT THE AUTHOR

Martin Schwabacher is the author of more than twenty books for young people, including *Elephants*, *Bears*, and *Butterflies* in the Animals Animals series. He is also a writer for the American Museum of Natural History, where he has contributed to the museum's permanent halls, exhibitions, online courses, and Web sites. He lives in New York City with his wife Melissa McDaniel, a children's book writer and editor, and their daughter Iris.

INDEX

Page numbers for illustrations are in **boldface.**